The Riddle of
the Rosetta Stone

The Riddle of the Rosetta Stone

KEY TO ANCIENT EGYPT

Illustrated with Photographs, Prints, and Drawings

JAMES CROSS GIBLIN

HarperTrophy®
A Division of HarperCollins*Publishers*

Library of Congress Cataloging-in-Publication Data

Giblin, James.
    The riddle of the Rosetta Stone : key to ancient Egypt ; illustrated
with photographs and prints / James Cross Giblin
        p.   cm.
    Includes bibliographical references and index.
    Summary: Describes how the discovery and deciphering of the
Rosetta Stone unlocked the secrets of Egyptian hieroglyphs.
    ISBN 0-690-04797-5. — ISBN 0-690-04799-1 (lib. bdg.)
    ISBN 0-06-446137-8 (pbk.)
    1. Egyptian language—Writing, Hieroglyphic—Juvenile literature.
2. Rosetta Stone—Juvenile literature.   [1. Rosetta Stone.
2. Egyptian language—Writing, Hieroglyphic.]   I. Title.
PJ1097.G5   1990   89-29289
493'.1—dc20   CIP
                                                        AC

Illustrations of hierogliphs on pp. 14, 34, 37, 39, 49, 50, 52, 54, 55, 58
© 1990 by Patricia Tobin

Frontispiece: Entrance to the ancient city of Luxor. Engraving by
Dominique Vivant Devon. Courtesy of the New York Public Library.

18 19 20 SCP 21

ACKNOWLEDGMENTS

I want to thank the following individuals and institutions for their help in providing research material and illustrations:

Sue Alexander
The British Museum, London
The Metropolitan Museum of Art, New York
Musée National du Louvre, Paris
The New York Public Library
Jeanne Prahl
The Wilbour Library of Egyptology,
    The Brooklyn Museum

Special thanks to Hilary Wallis and Joanne Federocko of Houghton Mifflin Company, who first suggested that I write about the Rosetta Stone, and to Barbara Fenton of HarperCollins, who believed the material had the makings of a book.

—J.C.G.

ALSO BY JAMES CROSS GIBLIN

LET THERE BE LIGHT: A BOOK ABOUT WINDOWS

FROM HAND TO MOUTH: OR, HOW WE INVENTED KNIVES, FORKS, SPOONS, AND CHOPSTICKS & THE TABLE MANNERS TO GO WITH THEM

MILK: THE FIGHT FOR PURITY

THE TRUTH ABOUT SANTA CLAUS

CHIMNEY SWEEPS: YESTERDAY AND TODAY

THE SKYSCRAPER BOOK

To the memory of my father,
Edward Kelley Giblin,
who taught himself six languages

A NOTE ABOUT THE ILLUSTRATIONS

The engravings in the book are by Dominique Vivant Denon, a member of Napoleon's Egyptian expedition. They illustrated Denon's book, *Travels in Upper and Lower Egypt*, which was published in France in 1829 and reprinted widely in other countries.

Denon's engravings appeared a decade before the invention of photography. Consequently, they provided many Europeans and Americans with their first glimpse of Egypt's ancient temples and monuments. The author found the pictures in a first-edition copy of Denon's book at The New York Public Library, and obtained prints for reproduction here.

CONTENTS

The Riddle of
the Rosetta Stone

I

The Mysterious Hieroglyphs

The scene: The Egyptian Sculpture Gallery of the British Museum in London. The time: Now.

Near the entrance to the long, high-ceilinged room stand two magnificent granite statues of Pharaoh Amenophis III, who ruled Egypt about 1400 B.C. Farther on is a colossal head of Pharaoh Ramesses II dating back to 1250 B.C. And beyond it, resting on a simple base, is a slab of black basalt, a volcanic rock.

Next to the statues and the head, the slab seems unimpressive at first glance. It is roughly the size of a tabletop—three feet nine inches long, two feet four and a half inches wide, and eleven inches thick. But many experts would say that this rather small piece of rock was more valuable than any of the larger objects in the

Left: Statue of Pharaoh Amenophis III, circa 1400 B.C. *Reproduced by Courtesy of the Trustees of the British Museum.*

Above: Head of Pharaoh Ramesses II, circa 1250 B.C. *Reproduced by Courtesy of the Trustees of the British Museum.*

The Rosetta Stone on display in the British Museum's Egyptian Sculpture Gallery. *Reproduced by Courtesy of the Trustees of the British Museum.*

room. For it is the famed Rosetta Stone, which gave nineteenth-century scholars their first key to the secrets of ancient Egypt.

What makes this stone so special? Step closer, and you'll see. Spotlights pick out markings carved into the surface of the stone, and close up you can tell that these marks are writing. At the top are fourteen lines of hieroglyphs—pictures of animals, birds, and geometric shapes. Below them you can make out thirty-two lines written in an unfamiliar script. And below that, at the bottom of the slab, are fifty-four more lines written in the letters of the Greek alphabet.

Before the Rosetta Stone was discovered in 1799, no one knew how to read Egyptian hieroglyphic writing. Its meaning had been lost for almost 1400 years. But countless visitors to Egypt over the centuries had tried to decipher the mysterious symbols. This is the story of their attempts, and of how the Rosetta Stone finally enabled scholars to unlock the Egyptian past.

The story begins in the seventh century A.D., when Greek scholars visiting Egypt first called the symbols "hieroglyphs." They gave them that name, which means "sacred carvings" in Greek, because they found so many of them on the walls of Egyptian tombs and temples.

Close-up of the hieroglyphic writing on the Rosetta Stone. *Reproduced by Courtesy of the Trustees of the British Museum.*

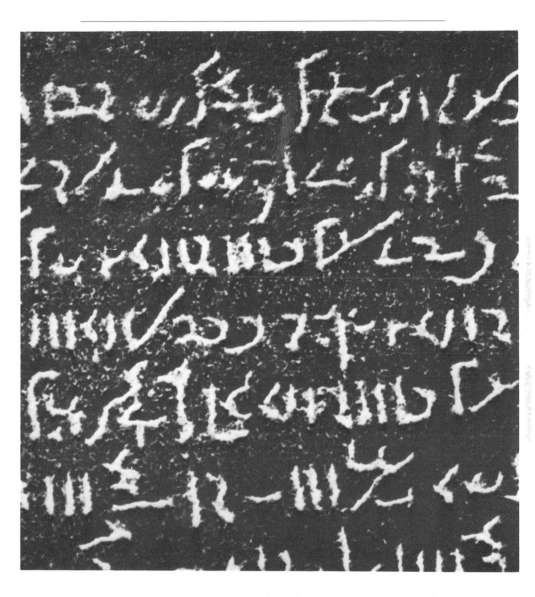

Part of the passage written in the other Egyptian script on the Rosetta Stone. *Reproduced by Courtesy of the Trustees of the British Museum.*

A section from the Greek passage on the Rosetta Stone. *Reproduced by Courtesy of the Trustees of the British Museum.*

As the Greeks sailed up the Nile River to the ancient cities of Memphis and Thebes, they asked native after native what the hieroglyphs meant. Not even the oldest Egyptians could tell them, for the language expressed in the hieroglyphs had already been dead for several hundred years. It had been replaced by Coptic, the language spoken by Christian Egyptians. And Coptic, in turn, was replaced by Arabic after the Arabs conquered Egypt in A.D. 642. By the time the visitors from Greece arrived, no living Egyptian knew how to read the hieroglyphic writing of his ancestors.

Frustrated in their attempts to get someone to translate the hieroglyphs for them, the Greeks decided on their own that the symbols must be a kind of picture writing. Some thought the pictures were mystical devices used in ancient religious rites, whose meaning was known only to long-dead Egyptian priests.

Others stumbled on the correct definitions of a few hieroglyphs. No one knows exactly where the Greeks obtained this information. Some think it came from craftsmen who made good-luck charms based on ancient Egyptian designs and still knew what those symbols meant.

However they obtained it, the Greeks couldn't

Above: Fragment of a limestone frieze from above the entrance to the tomb of a high official. VII–VIII Dynasties, 2258–2225 B.C. *Courtesy of The Metropolitan Museum of Art, Gift of Egypt Exploration Fund, 1898.*

Right: Pharaoh Seti I makes an offering to the god Osiris. Wall relief from the Temple of Pharaoh Ramesses I at Abydos. The hieroglyphs on this relief, like many other Egyptian examples, read from top to bottom. XIX Dynasty, 1315–1298 B.C. *Courtesy of The Metropolitan Museum of Art, Gift of J. Pierpont Morgan, 1911.*

resist adding their own original "explanations" to the definitions. For example, a Greek writer named Horapollo said correctly that the picture of a goose stood for the word "son." But then he explained that this was because geese took special care of their young, which was completely inaccurate. He wrote that the image of a rabbit meant "open" because a rabbit's eyes never close—an equally false statement.

Horapollo offered an even more unlikely explanation of a hieroglyph drawn in the form of a vulture.

First, he said that it stood for the word "mother," which happened to be correct. Then his imagination took over, and he claimed that the hieroglyph also meant "a sight, or boundaries, or foreknowledge." He went on to explain why.

"The vulture means a mother since there is no male in this species of animal," Horapollo wrote. (Of course this was untrue!) "It stands for sight since of all animals the vulture has the keenest vision. It means boundaries because, when a war is about to break out, the vulture limits the place in which it will be fought by

Part of a legal document written in the Coptic language. *Courtesy of The Metropolitan Museum of Art, Rogers Fund, 1924.*

hovering over the area for seven days. And it stands for foreknowledge because, in flying over the battlefield, the vulture looks forward to the corpses the slaughter will provide it for food."

The writings of Horapollo circulated widely throughout Europe and influenced the study of hieroglyphs for centuries to come. No one questioned the Greek writer's explanations. Instead, European scholars accepted them as truths and put forward their own mistaken interpretations of the mysterious symbols.

Some of these scholars made otherwise significant contributions to the world's knowledge of ancient Egypt. A German priest of the 1600s, Athanasius Kircher, wrote the first grammar and vocabulary of Coptic, the language of Christian Egypt. These books were to prove of great value when the hieroglyphs were eventually deciphered.

But Kircher's ideas about the hieroglyphs themselves were even farther off the mark than those of Horapollo. Looking at a certain group of symbols—which actually stood for the name of a pharaoh—Kircher let his imagination run wild. Without any evidence to support him, he said that the hieroglyphs meant "The blessings of the god Osiris are to be procured by means of sacred ceremonies, in order that the benefits of the river Nile may be obtained."

From 1650 onward, Kircher produced several volumes of such nonsense. It earned him a reputation for being an expert on the hieroglyphs— a reputation that lasted, unfortunately, long after his death in 1680.

A few genuine advances in understanding the hieroglyphs were made during the 1700s. The French scholar C. J. de Guignes observed that groups of hieroglyphs in Egyptian texts were often enclosed by an oval outline, which he called a *cartouche.* "Cartouche" is a French word that originally meant a cartridge, and the line around the hieroglyphs had a similar shape. De Guignes guessed rightly that the cartouches in hieroglyphic inscriptions were intended to draw attention to important names, probably the names of Egyptian rulers.

Along with such insights, de Guignes advanced other ideas about the hieroglyphs that were as silly as any that had been proposed by Kircher or Horapollo. After comparing some Egyptian hieroglyphs with examples of Chinese picture writing, de Guignes announced that settlers from Egypt must have colonized China in ancient times. English students of the 1700s

A royal cartouche from the back of a statue of the late Ptolemaic period, 80–30 B.C. *Courtesy of The Metropolitan Museum of Art, Purchase, Lila Acheson Wallace Gift and Rogers Fund, 1981.*

went the Frenchman one better. They declared that it had happened the other way around: The ancient Egyptians had come from China!

None of these theories brought scholars any closer to a true understanding of the hieroglyphs. As the 1700s came to an end, their meaning was as much of a mystery as ever.

Travelers to Egypt gazed in awe upon the pyramids. But because they could not decipher the hieroglyphs, neither they nor the natives had any idea when the gigantic structures were built, or how. The travelers saw the ruins of ancient cities and palaces. But they did not know who had lived in them, or what their lives were like.

All the secrets of ancient Egypt—its history, its literature, its religious beliefs—remained hidden behind the lines of the mysterious hieroglyphs. And it looked as if they might stay there forever. Then, in 1798, something happened that seemed at first to have nothing to do with the puzzle of the hieroglyphs. The French general Napoleon Bonaparte invaded Egypt with an army of 38,000 soldiers.

France was at war with England, and Napoleon's main goal was to occupy Egypt and then attack British-held India. But like many Europeans of the time, Napoleon was also interested

Funerary papyrus of the Princess Entiu-ny found in the tomb of her mother, Queen Meryet-Amun, at Thebes. The princess is shown at the top of the papyrus, plowing with a team of cows and reaping the ripe grain. XXI Dynasty, circa 1025 B.C. *Courtesy of The Metropolitan Museum of Art, Rogers Fund, 1930.*

in learning more about Egypt itself. So, along with the soldiers, Napoleon brought with him to Egypt a party of 167 scholars and scientists. Their assignment: to study every aspect of the country and its history.

What neither Napoleon nor the scholars could guess was that their most important discovery would be an odd-shaped black slab with three different kinds of writing on it.

II

The Stone Is Found

The French invasion was a great success at first. Napoleon's army captured the city of Alexandria by storm on July 1, 1798, and rapidly overran the Nile Delta. As they marched past the pyramids, Napoleon turned to his men and said, "Soldiers, forty centuries are looking down upon you."

Napoleon entered the Egyptian capital, Cairo, on July 21. There he took over an elegant palace to serve as the headquarters for his scholars and scientists. They began work immediately and acquired the nickname "the donkeys" because of the donkeys they rode on their expeditions into the countryside.

While the scholars pursued their studies, the tide was turning against Napoleon. On August 1 the British surprised the French fleet at anchor near Alexandria and completely destroyed it. Now Napoleon, his army, and the scholars were trapped in the land the French had conquered.

For the next year, the army fended off attacks by the Turks, who had formerly ruled Egypt. The scholars took measurements of sphinxes, gathered botanical specimens, and made copies of the still-mysterious hieroglyphs they found everywhere. Then, in August 1799, Napoleon evaded the British naval blockade and returned with a few companions to France to deal with problems there.

The French army stayed behind in Egypt—and so did the scholars. In late August, shortly after Napoleon's departure, a large, heavy package arrived at the scholars' palace in Cairo. When they opened it, they found it contained a black stone slab covered with writing in three different scripts.

A note from a French army officer accompanied the package. He told the scholars that the stone had been unearthed in an old fort near the town of Rosetta, thirty-five miles north of Alexandria. French soldiers were tearing down a ruined wall in the fort when they came upon the slab. The top right and left corners were missing,

French scholars measuring a sphinx near Cairo. Engraving by Dominique Vivant Denon. *Courtesy of The New York Public Library.*

as was the bottom right corner. The soldiers had gone over the rest of the wall carefully in hopes of finding the missing pieces embedded in it, but with no luck.

The scholars labeled the slab the "Rosetta Stone" in honor of the place where it was found, and called in their language experts to examine it. As soon as they glimpsed the writing on the slab, the experts became tremendously excited. This was the first time they had ever seen hieroglyphs carved on the same stone with a passage written in the familiar letters of the Greek alphabet.

Except for the missing corner, the Greek passage seemed to be quite complete. One of the experts set to work at once to translate it into French. He discovered that it was a decree passed by a gathering of priests in the city of Memphis in 196 B.C. The decree praised the accomplishments of the thirteen-year-old pharaoh, Ptolemy V Epiphanes, on the first anniversary of his coronation.

That explained why the passage was carved in Greek. The Greek leader, Alexander the Great, had taken control of Egypt in 332 B.C., and after Alexander's death in 323 B.C. his general, Ptolemy, replaced him. From then until 30 B.C.,

Soldiers from Napoleon's army on parade in the town of Rosetta. Engraving by Dominique Vivant Denon. *Courtesy of The New York Public Library.*

when Rome conquered Egypt, a long line of pharaohs from the Ptolemy family ruled the country. The Ptolemys kept their Greek culture, including their language, but they also respected the customs and religious beliefs of the native Egyptians. So it was only natural for the priests' statement to have been carved in both Greek and Egyptian on the Rosetta Stone.

After the Greek passage had been translated, the scholars turned their attention to the Egyptian writing on the slab. First they studied the hieroglyphs. Then they puzzled over the second script. They had seen examples of it before on rolls of papyrus, the writing material the Egyptians used instead of paper. Deciding that it was a simpler form of Egyptian writing, the scholars called it *demotic*, meaning "of the people."

But what did the passages in Egyptian mean? Did they contain exactly the same message as the Greek passage? The last sentence of the Greek text said, "This decree shall be inscribed on a stela [slab] of hard stone in sacred [hieroglyphic] and native [demotic] and Greek characters," so it seemed clear that the inscription was the same in all three languages. That way, the priests' statement could be read by Egyptians who understood Greek, as well as by those who knew only

Full view of the Rosetta Stone. *Reproduced by Courtesy of the Trustees of the British Museum.*

one or both of the Egyptian languages. But the scholars were still far from being able to decipher either the hieroglyphs or the demotic writing.

Meanwhile, the French situation in Egypt was going from bad to worse. In the spring of 1801, British troops landed near Alexandria and a Turkish army marched into Egypt from Syria. Cairo fell to the Turks in June, and the French, under General Jacques Menou, retreated to Alexandria. With the army went the scholars and all the material they had gathered in Egypt, including the Rosetta Stone.

Besieged and outnumbered, the French were finally forced to surrender to the British in September 1801. As part of the settlement, the British ordered the scholars to hand over their treasures. The scholars protested. "Without us," they said, "this material is a dead language that neither you nor your scientists can understand." General Menou went so far as to claim that the Rosetta Stone was his personal property.

At last the British gave in and allowed the scholars to keep the bulk of their collections. But they insisted on taking the Rosetta Stone. Reluctantly, General Menou turned it over to the British general, Hutchinson. "You can have it," he said, "because you are the stronger of us two."

III
Clues to the Puzzle

Fortunately, the French had made a number of copies of the inscriptions on the Rosetta Stone. They did this by covering the surface of the Stone with printer's ink, laying a sheet of paper on it, and rolling rubber rollers over it until good, clear impressions were obtained.

These ink impressions were sent to France, where they were studied closely by many scholars. Each scholar was eager to be the first to decipher the mysterious hieroglyphs, but most of them began by focusing on the demotic inscription, the most complete passage on the slab.

Unlike the hieroglyphs, which were separate units, the demotic script was *cursive*, which means that the strokes of the letters in each word were joined like handwriting. The scholars

A religious text written in the demotic Egyptian script. Roman period, first century A.D. *Courtesy of The Metropolitan Museum of Art, Gift of Edward S. Harkness, 1931.*

guessed that demotic was written with an alphabet, like Western languages. Once they discovered that alphabet, they thought the demotic script would be easier to translate than the pictorial hieroglyphs.

One of the French experts, Sylvestre de Sacy, started with the proper names in the Greek passage and tried to find their equivalents in the demotic version. He believed that, after he'd singled out the names, he would be able to identify the demotic letters in each of them. With these letters in hand, he could then go on to translate other names and words in the demotic passage.

But the process proved to be much more difficult than de Sacy had anticipated. He succeeded in isolating the groups of demotic letters for the names of Ptolemy and Alexander, but found it impossible to identify the individual letters in the names. Eventually he gave up, saying, "The problem is too complicated, scientifically insoluble."

A pupil of de Sacy's, the Swedish diplomat Johan Akerblad, made better progress. Akerblad managed to locate in the demotic passage all the proper names that occurred in the Greek. From them he constructed a "demotic alphabet" of twenty-nine letters, almost half of which later proved to be correct. He went on to demonstrate that the signs used to write the names were also used to write ordinary words like "him," "his," "temple," and "love."

These were impressive achievements. But Akerblad's success in identifying so many demotic characters now led him to make a serious mistake. He became convinced that the demotic script was entirely alphabetic. From then on Akerblad, and other scholars like him, made no further progress in deciphering the demotic passage on the Stone.

In the meantime, the Stone itself had been shipped to England in 1802. There, by order of King George III, it was housed in the British Museum and copies of the writing on the Stone were made available to interested English scholars. In 1814 one of these copies came to the attention of a well-known scientist, Dr. Thomas Young. Immediately his curiosity was aroused.

Young had learned to read before he was two, and by the age of twenty had mastered a dozen foreign languages including Arabic, Persian, and Turkish. An inheritance from an uncle left him free to pursue his scientific interests. At various times, Young studied the habits of spiders, the surface features of the moon, and diseases of the chest. Then, intrigued by the challenge of the Rosetta Stone, he put aside his other studies and concentrated on attempting to decipher the writing on it. Young had read of de Sacy's and Akerblad's work in Paris, and was determined to succeed where they had failed.

Like the French scholars, Young focused first on the demotic section and compared it closely with the Greek passage. He noted that the word "king," or "pharaoh," occurred thirty-seven times in the Greek and could be matched only by a group of demotic characters that was repeated about thirty times.

Similarly, there were eleven mentions of the boy pharaoh, Ptolemy, in the Greek version. Young, like de Sacy and Akerblad before him, decided their demotic equivalent must be a group of characters that occurred fourteen times. Here is how the name Ptolemy looked in the demotic (it reads from right to left):

Young noticed that each time these demotic characters appeared, they were set off at both ends by lines like parentheses. He guessed that the lines were a simplified version of the oval cartouches that surrounded royal names in the hieroglyphs.

Within a few weeks, Young identified most of the groups of characters in the demotic passage that formed individual words. But after that he found it difficult to go further. He wrote to a friend: "You tell me that I shall astonish the world if I make out the demotic inscription on the Rosetta Stone. On the contrary, I think it astonishing that it should not have been made out already, and that I should find the task so difficult. . . . By far the greater part of the words I have ascertaincd with tolerable certainty, and some of the most interesting without the shadow of a doubt. But I can read very few of them alphabetically except the proper names which Akerblad read before. . . ."

Unable to make fresh progress in deciphering the demotic passage, Young turned his attention to the hieroglyphs on the Stone. The beginning of the hieroglyphic inscription was missing, but most of the final lines were complete. Young compared them carefully with the last lines in the demotic version, and made an important discovery. He explained it as follows:

"After completing my analysis, I observed that the characters in the demotic inscription, which expressed the words God, Immortal, Priests, and some others, had a striking resemblance to the corresponding hieroglyphs. And since none of these demotic characters could be reconciled to any imaginable alphabet, I could scarcely doubt that they were imitations of the hieroglyphics. . . ."

Why was this observation of Young's so important? Because it was the first time any scholar had guessed that the demotic script was not completely separate from the hieroglyphic. Instead, as Young correctly noted, the demotic was a simpler form of the hieroglyphic, one that must have been easier for ancient Egyptians to write.

Encouraged by the breakthrough he had made, Young soon established links between many of the demotic characters on the Stone and their hieroglyphic equivalents. Next he turned his attention to the only name in the hieroglyphic section that appeared in a royal cartouche. After comparing its position with the position of names in the demotic passage, he decided it must be a hieroglyphic representation of the name Ptolemy.

In the sixth line of the hieroglyphic text, the symbols in the cartouche looked like this:

(For ease in reading, the direction of the writing in the above and later examples reads from left to right. It is a mirror image of the writing on the Rosetta Stone which, like most Egyptian writing, reads from right to left.)

In the same line, and again in the fourteenth line, Young found the same symbols repeated, but with additions. Here is how the longer cartouche appeared in the sixth line:

Young had already noted that there were variations in the way the name Ptolemy was spelled in the demotic text. From studying the Greek text, he also knew that the longer version of the Pharaoh's name contained additional titles, such as "Ruler of Upper and Lower Egypt." So he decided to concentrate on the symbols within the shorter cartouche, assuming they stood for Ptolemy's name alone.

Part of the royal cartouche of one of the Ptolemys. From the back of a statue of the late Ptolemaic period, 80–30 B.C. *Courtesy of The Metropolitan Museum of Art, Purchase, Lila Acheson Wallace Gift and Rogers Fund, 1981.*

Up until this time, everyone who tried to decipher the hieroglyphs thought they were a form
of picture writing. The image of a lion must
stand for a lion, or something associated with
the animal—his power or his strength. Now
Young made a leap of the imagination. It was
like the inspired hunches that have led to so
many of the great advances in science and tech-
nology over the ages.

Young knew that the Ptolemys were of Greek
descent, and the name "Ptolemy"—spelled
"Ptolemaios" in Greek and pronounced "Puh-
tol-uh-may-os"—was an unfamiliar one to the
Egyptians. So, instead of trying to picture it in
some way, mightn't the Egyptians have written
the name with hieroglyphic symbols that represented the sounds, or *phonetic values*, in it?
For example, mightn't the first symbol, ◻ , represent the sound for "P"—"Puh"?

Following through on his hunch, Young assigned letters representing sounds to the symbols in the royal cartouche, as follows:

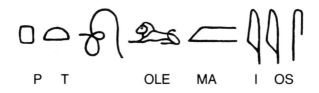

P   T   OLE   MA   I   OS

Thomas Young. *Courtesy of The New York Public Library.*

Young made several mistakes. He thought the third hieroglyph was part of the one for "T," whereas it actually stood for the vowel "O." The fourth hieroglyph, the lion, meant just "L," the fifth meant "M," and the last hieroglyph stood simply for "S." In other words, the spelling in Egyptian was "Ptolmis," not "Ptolemaios."

But Young got three out of the seven symbols right, which was a better score than any scholar before him had achieved.

Young published his findings in an article written for the 1819 supplement to the *Encyclopedia Britannica*. He continued to work on the problem of the hieroglyphs in the years that followed, but made little headway in deciphering additional names and words. Why? Largely because he was working under a false assumption.

Like countless other scholars over the centuries, Young still believed that most of the hieroglyphs must have a symbolic meaning. Only in special cases, such as foreign names, did he think that they were used to represent sounds.

Because of this mistaken belief, Young put roadblocks in his own path. However, he had laid a solid groundwork for others in their attempts to decipher the hieroglyphs. And a young Frenchman, Jean-François Champollion, was ready to take up the challenge where Young had left off.

IV

"I've Got It! I've Got It!"

Jean-François Champollion, like Thomas Young, had a gift for languages. The son of a bookseller, Champollion was born in a small town in southwestern France in 1790. At five he taught himself to read, and by the time he was ten he showed an unusual interest in the languages of the Middle East.

His older brother, Jacques-Joseph, encouraged this interest. Jacques-Joseph Champollion was a librarian who had long been fascinated by the Middle East himself. In fact, he had applied to go to Egypt with Napoleon's party of scholars—but had not been accepted.

When the younger Champollion was eleven, his brother took him to the southeastern French city of Grenoble to continue his education.

Jean-François Champollion (1790–1832). Portrait by Léon Cogniet, painted in 1831. *Courtesy of Musée du Louvre.*

There Champollion was introduced to the famous mathematician Jean-Baptiste Fourier. Fourier had accompanied Napoleon to Egypt, and he showed Champollion his collection of Egyptian antiquities, including a copy of the Rosetta Stone.

The ancient hieroglyphs fascinated the boy. He asked Fourier, "Can anyone read them?" The mathematician shook his head, and Champollion said, "I am going to do it. In a few years—when I am big."

By the time he was seventeen, Champollion had learned Greek, Hebrew, Arabic, Sanskrit, Persian, and other Near Eastern languages, as well as English, German, and Italian. Soon he added Coptic to the list by studying Kircher's grammar and vocabulary. Champollion believed that the Coptic language, which was written with the letters of the Greek alphabet, might have preserved some elements of ancient Egyptian writing.

After graduating in 1807 from the upper school in Grenoble, Champollion went to Paris. There he studied with Sylvestre de Sacy, the scholar who had attempted to decipher the writings on the Rosetta Stone a few years earlier.

Unlike Thomas Young, Champollion was very

poor. He lived in a tiny attic room and often had to write his brother in Grenoble for money. But no matter how difficult his living conditions were, Champollion never gave up his dream of being the first to discover the meaning of the hieroglyphs. He worked on them in his spare time, even after returning to Grenoble and taking a job as a teacher.

For many years Champollion's progress was blocked because, like de Sacy and earlier scholars, he believed the hieroglyphs represented things, not sounds. Then, in 1822, he reversed his position. Some of Champollion's rivals suggested that he had gotten the idea from Thomas Young's *Encyclopedia Britannica* article. There the English scholar explained how the hieroglyphs in Ptolemy's name stood for sounds. Champollion hotly denied these suggestions, claiming that he had arrived at his new position entirely on his own.

However the change came about, it provided Champollion with a new key to the puzzle of the hieroglyphs. He soon made use of it to go a step beyond Young and establish his own worth as a scholar once and for all.

In order to prove his theory about sounds correct, Champollion needed to identify a second

name that contained some of the same hieroglyphs as Ptolemy's. There weren't any on the
Rosetta Stone, so Champollion turned to copies
of hieroglyphic inscriptions from other Egyptian
monuments and temples. But no matter how
many copies he examined, he couldn't locate a
name that met his requirements.

As time passed, Champollion became more
and more frustrated. Then one day a colleague
sent him a copy of an inscription that had been
found in the ruins of a temple on the Nile River
island of Philae. Written in both hieroglyphs and
Greek, the inscription was a royal decree issued
by Pharaoh Ptolemy VII and his Queen, Cleopatra II. (This was not the famous Cleopatra, but
an earlier one.)

The Greek forms of Ptolemy and Cleopatra,
like the English, had several letters in com-
mon. However, Champollion corrected Thomas
Young's mistake and spelled the first name as
"Ptolmis." He also knew that Cleopatra began
with a "K" in Greek rather than a "C." Now it
was up to the French scholar to show whether
or not there was a duplication of hieroglyphs
in the Egyptian version of the names. He lined
up the two groups of symbols and made a com-
parison.

View of the island of Philae. Engraving by Dominique Vivant Denon. *Courtesy of The New York Public Library.*

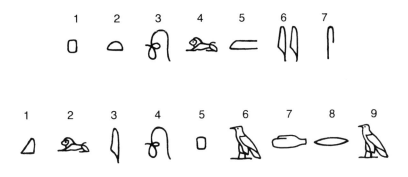

At once it was apparent that three of the hieroglyphs found in the name Ptolemy—the first, third, and fourth—could also be found in their correct places in the name Cleopatra—the fifth, fourth, and second respectively.

Moreover, the symbol that Champollion decided must stand for "A" in Cleopatra appeared where it should in the sixth place and again at the end. Rightly, neither this hieroglyph nor those that he realized must represent "K," "E," and "R" appeared in the name Ptolemy. Nor did the symbols for "M," "I," and "S" appear in the name Cleopatra.

The only hieroglyph that confused Champollion was the one for "T," which was different in the two names. (Later he learned that this represented a difference in pronunciation, for the Egyptians pronounced the "T" in Cleopatra like a "D.")

Having completed his analysis, Champollion assigned letters to all of the hieroglyphs:

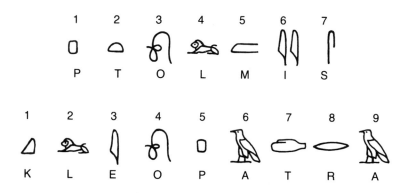

As soon as the last letter was in place, the young Frenchman rushed out of his apartment and ran to the nearby library where his brother was working. "I've got it! I've got it!" he shouted—and fainted.

Champollion had every reason to be excited. He had confirmed that more than one Greek name was expressed phonetically by the hieroglyphs. And he now knew a dozen different hieroglyphic symbols with which he could go about deciphering other Egyptian names and words.

He began with another cartouche from the same inscription and numbered each of the hieroglyphs in it.

Marble statuette of one of the Queen Cleopatras, possibly Cleopatra II. 206–30 B.C. *Courtesy of The Metropolitan Museum of Art, Gift of Joseph W. Drexel, 1889.*

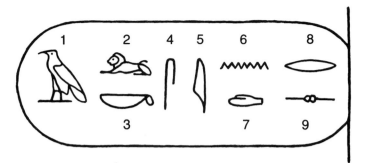

Of the nine symbols, Champollion already knew numbers 1, 2, 4, 5, 7, and 8. When he lined up all the numbers and put the corresponding letters beneath them, he got the following arrangement:

1 2 3 4 5 6 7 8 9
A L   S E   T R

Immediately Champollion thought of the one Greek leader whose name might be identified with this particular combination of letters. It was Alexander the Great, spelled "Alexandros" in Greek, and apparently represented as "Alksentrs" in hieroglyphs.

Champollion filled in the gaps in the arrangement:

1 2 3 4 5 6 7 8 9
A L K S E N T R S

Alabaster portrait bust of Alexander the Great. Probably from the first century B.C. *Courtesy of The Brooklyn Museum, Charles Edwin Wilbour Fund.*

Next he assigned letters to each of the hiero-glyphs in the cartouche:

Now he had three more signs to add to his list, those that stood for "K," "N," and "S." (He guessed, and rightly so, that the new hieroglyphs for "K" and "S" indicated that these sounds were pronounced differently in the name "Alksentrs" than they were in the royal names he had de-ciphered earlier.)

Working steadily, Champollion in the next month deciphered more than eighty cartouches. He succeeded in reading the names of all the Greek and Roman leaders who had ruled Egypt since the time of Alexander. He also translated the various titles adopted by these monarchs—"Caesar," "Great King," "Beloved of the Gods," etc. They added to his ever-growing list of iden-tifiable hieroglyphs, which soon numbered more than one hundred.

Still, a question nagged at Champollion. He had deciphered many cartouches from the period when Greek pharaohs ruled Egypt. But what about the three thousand years of Egyptian history before Alexander the Great conquered the country? Did the hieroglyphs written then stand for sounds like those written in the Egypt of the Ptolemys?

Champollion had a chance to resolve this question when a fellow scholar sent him copies of some inscriptions from a temple that had been built long before the time of the Ptolemys. The inscriptions included a number of royal cartouches. As he studied them, Champollion's attention was drawn to one that contained several familiar hieroglyphs:

He saw at once that the right-hand hieroglyph was a double form of the letter "S" from the name Ptolemy. The middle hieroglyph was unknown to him, but he guessed that the two at the left symbolized the sun.

From his studies of Coptic, Champollion knew that the Egyptian word for "sun" was pro-

Side of a door from a temple dedicated to Ramesses II at Thebes. The Pharaoh's cartouche can be seen in several places. In this instance his name is spelled Rameses instead of Ramesses. XIX Dynasty, 1315–1298 B.C. *Courtesy of The Metropolitan Museum of Art, Gift of Edward S. Harkness, 1913.*

nounced *rah*. He wrote down the first two letters of that sound, RA. Next he put a question mark for the unknown middle hieroglyph. Then, at the end, he wrote SS, the sound of the last two hiero-glyphs.

He studied the combination: RA ? SS. Sud-denly he remembered a famous pharaoh whose name appeared in ancient Greek chronicles and also in the Biblical Book of Exodus: Rameses, or Ramesses. Could this be a hieroglyphic repre-sentation of Ramesses' name?

To confirm this hunch, Champollion turned to the writings on the Rosetta Stone. There the unknown sign occurred, again in combination with ⌐ , as part of a group of hieroglyphs that correspond to the word "birthday" in the Greek passage. This made Champollion think at once of the Coptic word for "give birth," which was pronounced *mes*. He put that sound in place of the question mark, and there the name was: Ra-messes, "The Child of Ra."

(Champollion assumed there was an extra "E" for pronunciation's sake between the double "S" at the end of the name, and later studies proved he was right.)

Champollion had successfully deciphered one of the cartouches on the temple inscription, but what about the others? Would his methods work as well with them? To test them, he turned to a second cartouche, which contained the following hieroglyphs:

He recognized immediately that the last two hieroglyphs were the same as two in Ramesses and read "mes." They were accompanied by the figure of a bird, an ibis. Champollion knew from reading ancient Greek books that the ibis was the symbol of Thoth, the Egyptian god of learning and magic. He decided the three hieroglyphs must represent the name of Thothmes, the "Child of Thoth," a pharaoh who ruled Egypt from 1501 to 1447 B.C.

As he thought about the hieroglyphs in Thothmes' and Ramesses' names, Champollion realized their significance. It went far beyond the names themselves and gave him an insight into the entire system of hieroglyphic writing. For the names revealed that hieroglyphs were not simply representations of sounds. Nor did they have an exclusively symbolic meaning, as Thomas Young and other scholars had long be-

Coffin, covered with hieroglyphic inscriptions, of a high official during the reign of Thothmes IV. XVIII Dynasty, circa 1400–1390 B.C.
Courtesy of The Brooklyn Museum, Charles Edwin Wilbour Fund.

lieved. Instead, they were a combination of the two.

Champollion announced his discovery in a ground-breaking book about hieroglyphs published in 1824. In it he called ancient Egyptian writing a complex system that was "symbolical and phonetic in the same text, the same phrase, the same word."

Champollion must have felt an immense pride when he wrote that. All his years of painstaking and often frustrating attempts at deciphering had been rewarded. "I am going to do it," he had said as a boy when the mathematician Fourier showed him a copy of the Rosetta Stone. Now he had succeeded.

V
Ancient Egypt Revealed

In the next few years following the publication of his book, Champollion deciphered many more hieroglyphs. He was named "Keeper of the Egyptian Collections" in Paris in recognition of his accomplishments. Then, in 1829, he got what he had always wanted. With the backing of the French government, he journeyed to Egypt to see the ancient hieroglyphic inscriptions for himself.

A party of fourteen, including several artists and architects, accompanied Champollion. Deciding to dress like natives, they wore turbans on their heads, gold-embroidered jackets, and yellow boots. His friends said Champollion, who had a swarthy complexion, "looked more Egyptian than many of the Egyptians we met."

Entrance to the ancient city of Luxor. Engraving by Dominique Vivant Denon. *Courtesy of The New York Public Library.*

The group traveled up the Nile in two boats, stopping along the way to copy inscriptions on temples and monuments. After voyaging as far south as Nubia, they came back downstream to the ancient cities of Luxor and Thebes. At Thebes they camped in the Valley of the Kings, surrounded by the tombs of many pharaohs including Ramesses VI.

Following a visit to the ruins of Karnak near Thebes, Champollion wrote in his journal: "At last I have visited the palace, or rather the city, of monuments, Karnak. . . . No nation on earth, ancient or modern, has ever conceived architecture on so noble and vast a scale. . . . The Egyptians of old thought like men a hundred feet high."

But it was at Dendera that Champollion and his companions had their most thrilling experience of the trip. They came ashore on a brightly moonlit night, and after a two-hour march finally reached the Temple of Dendera with its gigantic columns.

"I will not try to describe the impression that the temple, and in particular its portico, made on us," Champollion wrote. "The separate dimensions of the structure can be measured, but it is quite impossible to give an idea of the whole.

We stayed there two hours, filled with ecstasy. Led by our native guide, we wandered through the halls and tried to read the inscriptions on the outside in the glittering moonlight."

Champollion spent almost a year and a half in Egypt. On his return home to Paris, he began the huge job of deciphering and organizing all the material he had gathered. Sad to say, he did not live to see the fruits of his labor. On March 4, 1832, while preparing the results of the expedition for publication, he collapsed and died after a series of strokes. He was only forty-one.

Champollion's contributions to the world's knowledge of ancient Egypt did not end with his death, however. Working from Champollion's notes, his brother Jacques-Joseph completed the *Egyptian Grammar* and *Egyptian Dictionary* that Champollion had started. The books were published in several volumes during the 1830s and 1840s, and were warmly welcomed by most scholars in France, Germany, England, and other countries.

A few experts challenged Champollion's methods and clung to the notion that the hieroglyphs had a purely symbolic meaning. But Champollion's defenders, after further studies, proved his approach correct beyond any doubt.

View of Karnak. Engraving by Dominique Vivant Denon. *Courtesy of The New York Public Library.*

Between the time Champollion's books appeared and the end of the nineteenth century, thousands of rolls of papyrus and copies of temple and tomb inscriptions were brought to Europe and America. There scholars, using the deciphering methods Champollion had pioneered, traced the entire history of writing in Egypt. They discovered it had begun about 3100 B.C. when images of important people were first accompanied by hieroglyphs of their names or titles. By 2500 B.C. complete sentences began to appear on tomb inscriptions, along with lists of offerings to the Egyptian gods.

Only those Egyptians who needed the knowledge for their professions learned how to read and write. These included government officials, doctors, and priests, as well as the scribes who did the actual writing on papyrus and stone.

The schooling of a scribe began at age five or six and was usually completed by age sixteen. Through long, hard hours of practice, the student learned to paint or carve more than six hundred different hieroglyphs. He also learned how to write in *hieratic*, a flowing form of hieroglyphic writing in which the individual symbols were joined.

Statuette of a scribe reading a papyrus scroll. XVIII Dynasty, 1580–1350 B.C. *Courtesy of The Metropolitan Museum of Art, Anonymous Gift, 1931.*

Scribes generally used the hieratic form when they were writing on papyrus, and hieroglyphs when they were carving inscriptions in plaster or limestone. Later, in about 700 B.C., hieratic writing was simplified further and became the form known as demotic. It was in demotic, of course, that one of the passages on the Rosetta Stone was carved.

Once they had mastered the three kinds of Egyptian writing, nineteenth-century scholars had the key to more than three thousand years of Egyptian history. Within a few decades, they compiled an accurate list of all the pharaohs who had ruled Egypt, from Narmer in 3000 B.C. to Cleopatra VII in 30 B.C. They discovered long-lost masterpieces of ancient Egyptian literature. And, by reading bills of sale, shop inventories, and personal letters, they reconstructed what daily life in ancient Egypt was like for everyone from a slave to a king.

Although he didn't live to share in these discoveries, Champollion had looked forward to them. Soon after his return from Egypt, he had written: "Egypt is always herself, at all stages in her history. Going back through the centuries, we see her always shining with the same brilliance, and the only thing we lack to satisfy our

Fragment of a legal document, perhaps a police report, written in the hieratic form of the ancient Egyptian language. XX–XXI Dynasty, 1200–945 B.C. *Courtesy of The Metropolitan Museum of Art.*

Model of a scribe's palette, with pens and two ink wells carved in relief. This model was found in the tomb of a scribe in lower Egypt, and is inscribed with prayers for the soul of its dead owner. XVIII Dynasty, 1580–1350 B.C. *Courtesy of The Metropolitan Museum of Art, Anonymous Gift, 1930.*

curiosity is a knowledge of the origin and growth of civilization itself."

Champollion helped to provide the world with that knowledge, which scholars today are still adding to. And it all began with the Rosetta Stone.

Afterword:
The Message on the Stone

It took more than a hundred years, and the efforts of many scholars, to translate all three passages of writing on the Rosetta Stone.

As we have seen, the first translation of the Greek passage into French was made shortly after the discovery of the Stone in 1799. The earliest translation into English was done in 1802, following the arrival of the Stone in England.

De Sacy, Akerblad, Young, Champollion, and others all made some progress in translating the demotic passage. But the first scholar who fully understood the symbols in the demotic text was a German, Heinrich Karl Brugsch, who published a translation of it, with commentary, in 1850. An even more thorough version was published by another German scholar, Dr. J. J. Hess, in 1902.

The hieroglyphic passage took the longest to translate, partly because the hieroglyphs were the least understood of the three languages, and partly because so much of the text was missing. Champollion succeeded in deciphering a large part of the passage, but the meaning of many hieroglyphs was still unknown when he did his major work in the 1820s.

Another, more complete copy of the same decree that appeared on the Stone was found on a slab at Philae in 1848. Fuller translations of the hieroglyphic text soon followed. A Latin version came out in 1851, a French one in 1867, and an English one in 1871. But many of the hieroglyphs on this slab were missing also, so only a few words and phrases could be added to what was already known from the Rosetta Stone.

Then, in 1887, yet another copy of the decree—this one almost intact—was unearthed in the ruins of a temple in Lower Egypt. Now, for the first time, scholars had a version of the hieroglyphic text that they could compare line-for-line with the Greek and demotic versions.

New translations of the hieroglyphic text were made in France and Germany, and an excellent English one appeared in 1904. A few sections still remain unclear, though. This makes present-day experts hope that an even more complete copy of the hieroglyphic inscription may yet be found, somewhere in Egypt.

Here are some excerpts from the decree; they give a sense of its content and the style in which it was written. These excerpts come from the English translation of the Greek passage that was made in the early 1800s.

DECREE. *There being assembled the Chief Priests and Prophets and those who enter the inner shrine for the robing of the gods, and the Fan-bearers and the Sacred Scribes and all the other priests from the temples throughout the land who have come to meet the king at Memphis, for the feast of the assumption by* PTOLEMY, THE EVER-LIVING, THE BELOVED OF PTAH, THE GOD EPIPHANES EUCHA-RISTOS, *of the kingship in which he succeeded his father,*

Limestone bust of a Ptolemaic pharaoh, possibly Ptolemy V. Circa 100–30 B.C. *Courtesy of The Metropolitan Museum of Art, Rogers Fund, 1910.*

they being assembled in the temple in Memphis on this day declared:

Whereas King **PTOLEMY,** *the son of King Ptolemy and Queen Arsinoe, has been a benefactor both to the temples and to those who dwell in them, as well as all those who are his subjects, and being benevolently disposed toward the gods, has dedicated to the temples revenues in money and grain and has undertaken much outlay to bring Egypt into prosperity, and has been generous with all his own means;*

and of the revenues and taxes levied in Egypt some he has wholly remitted and others has lightened, in order that the people and all the others might be in prosperity during his reign;

and whereas those who were in prison and those who were under accusation for a long time, he has freed of the charges against them;

and whereas he has directed that the gods shall continue to enjoy the revenues of the temples and the yearly allowances given to them, both of grain and money, and whereas he directed also, with regard to the priests, that they should pay no more as the tax for admission to the priesthood than was appointed them throughout his father's reign and until the first year of his own reign;

and whereas he has directed that impressment for the navy shall no longer be employed;

and whereas he provided that cavalry and infantry forces and ships should be sent out against those who invaded Egypt by sea and by land, laying out great sums in money and grain in order that the temples and all those who are in the land might be in safety;

in return for which things the gods have given him health, victory, and power, and all other good things, and he and his children shall retain the kingship for all time.

WITH PROPITIOUS FORTUNE: *It was resolved by the priests of all the temples in the land to increase greatly the existing honors of King* PTOLEMY, *likewise those of his parents, and of his ancestors, and to set up in the most prominent place of every temple an image of the* EVER-LIVING *King* PTOLEMY, THE BELOVED OF PTAH, THE GOD EPIPHANES EUCHARISTOS, *an image which shall be called that of* "PTOLEMY, *the defender of Egypt*," *beside which shall stand the principal god of the temple, handing him the weapon of victory;*

and that the priests shall pay homage to the images three times a day, and put upon them the sacred garments, and perform the other usual honors such as are given to the other gods in the Egyptian festivals;

and to establish for King PTOLEMY, THE GOD EPIPHANES EUCHARISTOS, *sprung of King Ptolemy and Queen Arsinoe, a statue and golden shrine in each of the temples, and to set it up in the inner chamber with the other shrines; and in the great festivals in which the shrines are carried in procession the shrine of the* GOD EPIPHANES EUCHARISTOS *shall be carried in procession with them;*

and private individuals shall also be allowed to set up the aforementioned shrine and have it in their homes, in order that it may be known to all that the people of Egypt magnify and honor the GOD EPIPHANES EUCHARISTOS *the king, according to the law.*

This decree shall be inscribed on a stela [slab] of hard stone in sacred [hieroglyphic] and native [demotic] and Greek characters and set up in each of the first, second, and third rank temples beside the image of the ever-living king.

Bibliography

(Those titles marked with an asterisk were written for young people.)

Andrews, Carol. *The British Museum Book of the Rosetta Stone.* New York: Peter Bedrick Books, 1985.

Budge, Sir E. A. Wallis. *The Rosetta Stone in the British Museum.* London: The Religious Tract Society, 1929.

Casson, Lionel, and the editors of Time-Life Books. *Ancient Egypt.* New York: Time, Inc., 1965.

Ceram, C. W. *Gods, Graves, and Scholars: The Story of Archaeology.* Translated from the German by E. B. Garside and Sophie Wilkins. Second, revised edition. New York: Alfred A. Knopf, 1967.

Cleator, P. E. *Lost Languages.* New York: The John Day Company, 1961.

*Cottrell, Leonard. *Reading the Past: The Story of Deciphering Ancient Languages.* New York: Crowell-Collier Books, 1971.

Davies, W. V. *Egyptian Hieroglyphics.* Berkeley and Los Angeles: University of California Press/British Museum, 1987.

Fagan, Brian M. *The Rape of the Nile.* New York: Charles Scribner's Sons, 1975.

*Frimmer, Steven. *The Stones That Spoke: And Other Clues to the Decipherment of Lost Languages.* New York: G. P. Putnam's Sons, 1969.

Hobson, Christine. *The World of the Pharaohs.* New York: Thames and Hudson, 1987.

*Katan, Norma Jean, with Barbara Mintz. *Hieroglyphs: The Writing of Ancient Egypt.* New York: Atheneum (A Margaret K. McElderry Book), 1981.

*Payne, Elizabeth. *The Pharaohs of Ancient Egypt.* New York: Random House, 1964.

*Perl, Lila. *Mummies, Tombs, and Treasure: Secrets of Ancient Egypt.* New York: Clarion Books, 1987.

Quirke, Stephen, and Carol Andrews. *The Rosetta Stone, Facsimile Drawing,* with an introduction and translation. London: British Museum Publications, 1988.

*Scott, Joseph, and Lenore Scott. *Egyptian Hieroglyphs for Everyone: An Introduction to the Writing of Ancient Egypt.* New York: Thomas Y. Crowell, 1968.

Zehren, Erich. *The Crescent and the Bull: A Survey of Archaeology in the Near East.* Translated from the German by James Cleugh. New York: Hawthorn Books, Inc., 1962.

Besides the above books, I found immensely helpful the vast Egyptian Collection of The Metropolitan Museum of Art. Especially useful were the illuminated table texts on the history of Egyptian art and culture. The Egyptian galleries of The Brooklyn Museum, The Cleveland Museum of Art, and The Museum of Fine Arts in Boston also provided me with many insights and much additional information.

Index

Page numbers in *italic* type indicate illustrations.